LEVEL

3

Cleopatra

Barbara Kramer

NATIONAL
GEOGRAPHIC

Washington, D.C.

For Kinsey —B. K.

Not much is known about Cleopatra. Myths and legends about her have survived, but how much of them is true is unknown. Much of the early information about Cleopatra came from a book about Mark Antony called *Life of Antony*. The Greek historian Plutarch wrote it more than 100 years after Cleopatra died. Almost all images of Cleopatra's likeness made during her lifetime are gone. The coin with her likeness on page 6 is one of the only images of her that remains. The cover art shows what Cleopatra might have looked like at age 18, at the beginning of her reign as queen of Egypt. Although she was queen of Egypt, current research suggests that she was of Greek heritage, as she is portrayed on the cover. The art throughout this book depicts many different interpretations of Cleopatra.

The lotus flower, featured throughout the book, closes at night and opens during the day. In ancient Egypt, it became a symbol of the sun and creation. The yellow borders at the top of the pages illustrate a type of paper made from the stalks of the papyrus plants that grew wild along the Nile River.

Trade paperback ISBN: 978-1-4263-2137-5
Reinforced library binding ISBN: 978-1-4263-2138-2

Editor: Shelby Alinsky
Art Director: Callie Broaddus
Editorial: Snapdragon Books
Designer: YAY! Design
Photo Editor: Lori Epstein
Production Assistants: Sanjida Rashid and Rachel Kenny
Rights Clearance Specialist: Colm McKeveny
Manufacturing Manager: Rachel Faulise

The author and publisher gratefully acknowledge the expert content review of this book by Jennifer Houser Wegner, Ph.D., associate curator, Egyptian Section, Penn Museum, and the literacy review of this book by Mariam Jean Dreher, professor of reading education, University of Maryland, College Park.

Photo Credits

GI: Getty Images; NGC: National Geographic Creative
Cover, Patrick Faricy; 1, Kenneth Garrett/NGC; 3, Cleopatra VII (69–30 B.C.E.), famous queen of Egypt/Marble bust/Antikensammlung, Staatliche Museen, Berlin, Germany/Johannes Laurentius/bpk/Art Resource, NY; 4, SuperStock; 5 (UP), Michelangelo Buonarroti (1475–1564) Head of Cleopatra/Casa Buonarroti, Florence, Italy/Scala/Art Resource, NY; 5 (LO), Link, William (19–20th c.) Brooch in form of Cleopatra. 1902. Silver. Collection of the Newark Museum/Art Resource, NY; 6 (UP), Kenneth Garrett/NGC; 6 (LO), GraphicaArtis/Corbis; 8, Kenneth Garrett/NGC; 9, Universal History Archive/GI; 10, Christoph Gerigk/NGC; 11 (UP), GraphicaArtis/Corbis; 11 (LO), The Granger Collection, NYC—All rights reserved; 12 (UP), De Agostini/GI; 12 (LO), Federica Milella/SS; 13 (UP), De Agostini/GI; 13 (CTR), Alistair Duncan/Dorling Kindersley/GI; 13 (LO), Wrangel/Dreamstime; 14, Courtesy Royal Ontario Museum; 17, Cleopatra (69–30 B.C.) before Julius Caesar (100–44 B.C.)/engraving after the painting by Jean Léon Gérôme/The Granger Collection, NYC—All rights reserved; 19, The Granger Collection, NYC—All rights reserved; 20, Corbis; 21, DEA/A. Daglie Orti/De Agostini/GI; 23, Cortona, Pietro da (1596–1669) Caesar Leads Cleopatra Back to the Throne of Egypt./Musée des Beaux-Arts, Lyon, France/RMN-Grand Palais/Art Resource, NY; 25 (LE), George Steinmetz/NGC; 25 (RT), Late republican denarii with Mark Antony and Augustus Caesar/HIP/Art Resource, NY; 27, The Meeting of Anthony and Cleopatra, 41 B.C. Sir Lawrence Alma-Tadema (1836–1912)/Christie's Images/Corbis; 28, The Banquet of Cleopatra, 1743–1744/Giovanni Battista Tiepolo/National Gallery of Victoria, Melbourne, Australia/HIP/Art Resource, NY; 29, Bust of Mark Antony in the Museum of the Vatican/Corbis; 30, The Granger Collection, NYC—All rights reserved; 31, Brian Cahn/ZUMA Press/Corbis; 32 (UP), bumihills/SS; 32 (CTR), North Wind Picture Archives; 32 (LO), Louie Psihoyos/Corbis; 33 (UP), Bettmann/Corbis; 33 (CTR LE), sculpies/SS; 33 (CTR RT), An engraving of Act IV, Scene 8 from Antony & Cleopatra by William Shakespeare/Corbis; 33 (LO), Victoria and Albert Museum, London, Great Britain/V&A Images, London/Art Resource, NY; 34, NG Maps; 35, sculpies/SS; 36, Antony & Cleopatra, Egyptian Theater by Alexis van Hamme/Fine Art Photographic Library/Corbis; 38–39, The Battle of Actium by Neroccio de' Landi/North Carolina Museum of Art/Corbis; 39 (LO), The Granger Collection, NYC—All rights reserved; 40, Batoni, Pompeo (1708–1787)/La mort de Marc Antoine l'homme politique et général romain/Musée des Beaux-Arts/Art Resource, NY; 40–43 (LO border), marina_ua/SS; 41, Baader, Louis-Marie (1828–1920) The Death of Cleopatra/Musée des Beaux-Arts, Rennes, France/RMN-Grand Palais/Art Resource, NY; 43 (UP), Christoph Gerigk © Franck Goddio/Hilti Foundation; 43 (CTR), Christoph Gerigk © Franck Goddio/Hilti Foundation; 43 (LO), Kenneth Garrett/NGC; 44 (UP), Pakhnyushchy/SS; 44 (CTR), Foley, Margaret (1830–1877) Cleopatra/Smithsonian American Art Museum, Washington, DC, USA/Art Resource, NY; 44 (LO-A), pirtuss/SS; 44 (LO-B), O. Louis Mazzatenta/NGC; 44 (LO-C), Eugene Sergeev/SS; 44 (LO-D), The sun-boat or funeral boat of Pharaoh Cheops/Giza, Egypt/Erich Lessing/Art Resource, NY; 45 (UP), clubfoto/iStockphoto; 45 (CTR RT), Patrick Faricy; 45 (CTR LE), The Granger Collection, NYC—All rights reserved; 45 (LO), Elias H. Debbas II/SS; 46 (UP), The Granger Collection, NYC—All rights reserved; 46 (CTR LE), The Granger Collection, NYC—All rights reserved; 46 (CTR RT), NG Maps; 46 (LO LE), Nurse whispering to Phaedra, sarcophagus of Phaedra and Hippolytus/Archaeological Museum Istanbul/The Art Archive/Gianni Dagli Orti/Art Resource, NY; 46 (LO RT), De Agostini/GI; 47 (UP LE), The Granger Collection, NYC—All rights reserved; 47 (UP RT), Gaius Julius Caesar Octavianus/Rome, Italy/Album/Art Resource, NY; 47 (CTR LE), Cleopatra (69–30 B.C.) before Julius Caesar (100–44 B.C.)/engraving after the painting by Jean Léon Gérôme/The Granger Collection, NYC—All rights reserved; 47 (CTR RT), The Granger Collection, NYC—All rights reserved; 47 (LO LE), François Guenet/Art Resource, NY; 47 (LO RT), Universal Images Group Editorial/GI; top border, throughout, Jaywarren79/SS; vocabulary box art, Michal812/Dreamstime

National Geographic supports K–12 educators with ELA Common Core Resources. Visit natgeoed.org/commoncore for more information.

Table of Contents

Who Was Cleopatra?

Cleopatra was queen of Egypt more than 2,000 years ago. Today, she is still one of history's most famous queens. Books and plays have been written about her. Movies have been made about her life. Those stories show what writers *think* she was like. The truth is there are many things we do not know about Cleopatra.

Her letters and other writings were lost. Images and statues of her made during her lifetime are gone. They would have offered important clues about what Cleopatra was like. Without them, much of her life is a mystery.

a drawing of Cleopatra by Michelangelo

Elizabeth Taylor starred in the movie *Cleopatra* in 1963.

a modern pin that pictures Cleopatra

A Beauty Queen?

Some people have said Cleopatra was a great beauty. Others said she was pleasant looking but had a hooked nose and a pointed chin. It was the way she talked and acted that made her beautiful. This coin is one of the only images of Cleopatra from her time that has been found.

We do know that Cleopatra was smart, brave, and charming. She was still a teenager when she became queen of Egypt in 51 B.C.

In His Own Words

"The attraction of her person, joining with the charm of her conversation, and the character that attended all she said or did, was something bewitching."
—Plutarch, Greek historian

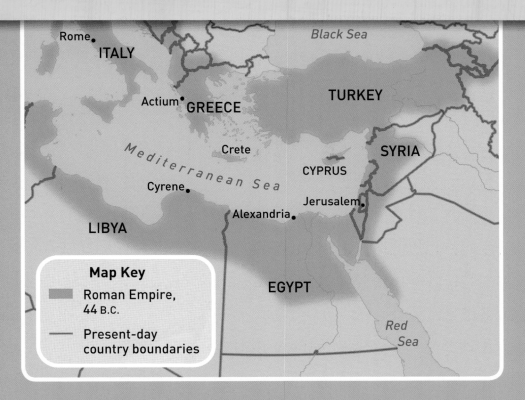

Rome.
ITALY

Black Sea

TURKEY

Actium• GREECE

Crete

SYRIA

Mediterranean Sea

CYPRUS

Cyrene•

Jerusalem•

Alexandria•

LIBYA

Map Key

Roman Empire,
44 B.C.

Present-day
country boundaries

EGYPT

Red
Sea

Egypt is in Africa. Its northern border is the Mediterranean (me-di-ter-RAY-nee-an) Sea. To the northwest was Rome. Today, Rome is a city in Italy. In Cleopatra's time, Rome was also the name of a large, powerful empire with a strong army. Roman leaders wanted to control the world. Yet for almost 20 years, Cleopatra kept Rome from taking over Egypt.

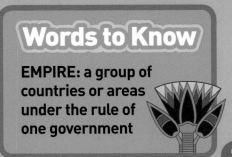

Words to Know

EMPIRE: a group of countries or areas under the rule of one government

7

Birth of a Queen

Cleopatra was born in the city of Alexandria, Egypt, in 69 B.C. Her ancestors, or family from earlier generations, were originally from Greece. But they had ruled Egypt for more than 250 years.

a statue that some believe shows Cleopatra's father, Ptolemy XII

That's a FACT! The calendar we use today began with the year A.D. 1. Cleopatra lived before that time. Her calendar *ended* in the year 1 B.C. On that calendar, the years were counted backward, like negative numbers on a number line, to the year 1 B.C. For example, Cleopatra was born in 69 B.C. She turned five years old in 64 B.C.

detail of a mosaic showing Alexander the Great in battle

Roman Numbers

Historians use Roman numbers as a way to tell Cleopatra's family members apart. In that numbering system, the capital letter I = 1, V = 5, and X = 10. Letters are added together to make larger numbers.

XII = 12
X + I + I = 12
10 + 1 + 1 = 12

A smaller letter placed in front of a large one means to subtract.

XIV = 14
X + (V – I) = 14
10 + (5 –1) = 14

The first person in Cleopatra's family to rule Egypt was named Ptolemy (TAHL-uh–mee). He arrived in Egypt with Alexander the Great, a king from northern Greece. Alexander took over Egypt in 332 B.C. Ptolemy was a general in his army. When Alexander died, Ptolemy became ruler of Egypt. Historians call him Ptolemy I (the first).

Alexandria was a center for learning. Scholars came from all over the world to study there. The city had the largest library in the world. It had thousands of scrolls written in many different languages.

Most girls did not go to school. It was different for Cleopatra. As a member of the ruling family, she got a good education. She studied history, science, medicine, and math. She read the work of important writers. She also learned to speak many languages.

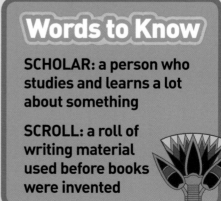

Words to Know

SCHOLAR: a person who studies and learns a lot about something

SCROLL: a roll of writing material used before books were invented

This marble statue is believed to be Cleopatra.

a picture by Harold Oakley of the famous Lighthouse of Alexandria

In His Own Words

"It was a pleasure merely to hear the sound of her voice, with which, like an instrument of many strings, she could pass from one language to another."
—Plutarch, Greek historian

In Her Time

When Cleopatra was a child growing up in Egypt, from about 68 to 52 B.C., life was very different from how it is now.

SCHOOL: Mothers taught their daughters to run a household. Education for boys meant training them for their careers. They usually did the same work as their fathers.

TOYS AND GAMES: Both boys and girls enjoyed playing ball games. They had toy animals and dolls carved from wood or made from clay. They also played board games. A game called senet used a checkered board.

TRANSPORTATION: The easiest way to travel was by boat or barge (barj) on the Nile River. It flowed north to the Mediterranean Sea. Most towns were built along the banks of the Nile.

THE LAND: Each year the Nile River flooded during Egypt's rainy season, from July to October. When the water went down, it left a layer of rich soil for growing fruits, vegetables, and grain.

MUSIC: Guests at parties and banquets were entertained with singing and dancing. Musicians played instruments such as lutes, lyres, and harps.

A Fight for Power

Cleopatra's father died in 51 B.C. He left his throne to Cleopatra and her younger brother, known by historians as Ptolemy XIII (the thirteenth). He was only 10 or 11 years old. He was not very interested in ruling a country. That gave Cleopatra freedom to rule the way she wanted.

But Ptolemy XIII's advisers did not want Cleopatra to have so much power. They helped Ptolemy take control of the throne. Cleopatra either left or was forced out of Alexandria. She went to the country of Syria (SEAR-ree-uh). There she raised a small army. By 48 B.C., she was ready to return to Alexandria to fight her brother and his advisers for the throne.

Some believe that this may be a statue of Cleopatra.

That's a FACT!

As queen of Egypt, Cleopatra became Cleopatra VII.

Words to Know

ADVISER: a person who gives advice about what should be done

A Sneaky Plan

Luck was on Cleopatra's side. Julius Caesar (JUE-lee-us SEA-zur), a powerful Roman general, had just arrived in Alexandria. He settled into the palace as an unwelcome guest.

Cleopatra wanted Caesar's help to win back the throne. But her brother's soldiers were guarding the palace. To talk to Caesar, she had to get past them.

One night, Cleopatra and a trusted friend sailed into Alexandria. It is not certain how Cleopatra got inside the palace. Legend (LEJ-und) says her friend rolled her up in a rug. Then he carried her into the palace as if the rug were a gift for Caesar.

Words to Know

LEGEND: a story from the past believed by many

This painting is by Jean-Léon Gérôme. In it, the artist shows what he thinks may have happened when Cleopatra spoke with Caesar. Next to Cleopatra is the rug in which she was supposedly hidden.

Cleopatra had the whole night to talk to Caesar. It did not go as she had hoped. People of that time did not believe a woman should rule a country without a king. Caesar wanted to end the fight between Cleopatra and her brother and make them co-rulers again.

Ptolemy XIII and his advisers did not like that idea. They wanted to get rid of Cleopatra. They could not do that with Caesar helping her. So they went to war against Caesar. After a hard fight, Caesar's soldiers defeated (dee-FEE-ted) Ptolemy's army. Ptolemy drowned in the Nile River.

Words to Know

DEFEAT: to win a victory over someone

CO-RULER: someone who rules together with another

a wood engraving of Julius Caesar from the 19th century

That's a FACT!

Caesar was 52 years old and an important general. Cleopatra was only 21, but she was smart. She could also talk easily to everyone she met. Caesar liked those things about her.

A Celebration

a painting of Cleopatra's boat on the Nile by Henri Pierre Picou

Caesar and Cleopatra celebrated their victory with a cruise. They floated down the Nile River in a long, flat boat called a barge. People lined up along the banks of the river to see them. The trip showed the people of Egypt that Cleopatra was queen again.

After a few weeks, Caesar went back to Rome. Before he left, he made Cleopatra a co-ruler with her youngest brother. He was about 12 years old. In history he is known as Ptolemy XIV (the fourteenth).

Queen and Goddess

People from Egypt believed their rulers were gods and goddesses. Cleopatra sometimes dressed to look like Isis, a powerful Egyptian goddess.

a wall painting of Isis from about 1360 B.C.

A Royal Son

In June, 47 B.C., Cleopatra gave birth to a son. She named him Ptolemy Caesar. He was named for Julius Caesar. To historians, he is known as Ptolemy XV (the fifteenth).

Caesar wanted Cleopatra to join him in Rome. A year later, in 46 B.C., she arrived with her son and her brother Ptolemy XIV. The Roman people did not welcome them. After all, Cleopatra was a queen from another country.

Rumors spread. People said Caesar planned to make himself king of the empire of Rome. Cleopatra would be his queen. But Caesar already had a wife. People also feared that Alexandria would replace the city of Rome as the empire's capital.

This painting from the 1600s of Caesar and Cleopatra is by Pietro da Cortona.

A Change in Power

Members of the Roman Senate then turned against Caesar. They stabbed him to death at a meeting on March 15, 44 B.C.

Cleopatra was no longer safe in Rome. She left the country with her son and her brother. Soon after they returned to Egypt, her brother disappeared. It is not clear what happened to him. Cleopatra made her three-year-old son her co-ruler. Once again, she was in control.

Words to Know

SENATE: the group that made laws in Rome

That's a FACT!

On the Roman calendar, March 15 was known as the Ides of March. Today, a popular saying is: "Beware the Ides of March." It is a warning of danger ahead.

Cleopatra and her son, Ptolemy Caesar

Mark Antony

Octavian

After Caesar's death, two men rose to power in Rome. They agreed to rule as a team. Mark Antony ruled the eastern part of the empire of Rome. Octavian (ock–TAY–vee–un) ruled the west.

Meeting the Queen

Egypt was a rich nation, and Rome had a strong army. Antony needed money to fight wars to take over new lands. Cleopatra wanted protection for Egypt from other countries. Antony believed they could help each other.

In 41 B.C., he traveled to the city of Tarsus in present-day Turkey. He sent messages asking Cleopatra to meet him there. She did not reply. She made him wait.

a painting of Cleopatra meeting Mark Antony by Sir Lawrence Alma-Tadema

Finally, she arrived on a barge trimmed with gold. It had purple sails and silver oars. Young women steered the barge and worked the sails' ropes. Young men fanned the queen to keep her cool.

This 1740s painting by Giovanni Battista Tiepolo is called "The Banquet of Cleopatra."

For the next four nights, Antony and Cleopatra feasted. They also talked about how they could help each other. Cleopatra returned to Alexandria, and Antony soon followed.

Antony and Cleopatra spent more time together. They played games and went hunting and fishing. Some nights they dressed as servants. Then they roamed the streets, knocking on doors and playing tricks on people.

In Rome, some of Antony's friends and family started a war with Octavian. They were defeated, but their actions created problems for Antony. He needed to let Octavian know he had nothing to do with that war.

sculpture of Mark Antony

On Her Own

In 40 B.C., Antony went back to Rome to make up with Octavian. Once again, they agreed to work as a team. To make their deal stronger, Antony married

a statue believed to be of Cleopatra from around 51 to 30 B.C.

Octavian's sister. It was a way for Antony to show that he was loyal to Octavian.

The news of Antony's marriage might have made Cleopatra sad. But she kept busy with the business of being queen. She met with leaders of other countries. She repaired temples and built ships for a stronger navy.

Words to Know

LOYAL: faithful or trusted

Some believe parts of this document were written by Cleopatra.

7 COOL FACTS About Cleopatra

1 The name Cleopatra means "glory of her father." On this stone tablet, Cleopatra's name is written using hieroglyphs, ancient Egyptian writing.

As a girl, Cleopatra had lessons in public speaking. She learned to talk to both small and large groups of people. **2**

3 Cleopatra was the only member of her family who learned to speak the Egyptian language. Other family members spoke only Greek. This photo shows the Egyptian language on part of an old scroll.

4 Legend says Cleopatra wrote about medicine and math and how to use makeup, but those scrolls have not been found.

5 Cleopatra was born more than 2,000 years after Egypt's famous pyramids were built.

In about A.D. 1623, William Shakespeare, a famous writer from England, wrote a play called *Antony and Cleopatra*. **6**

7 Cleopatra was the richest woman in the world during her time.

Trouble Ahead

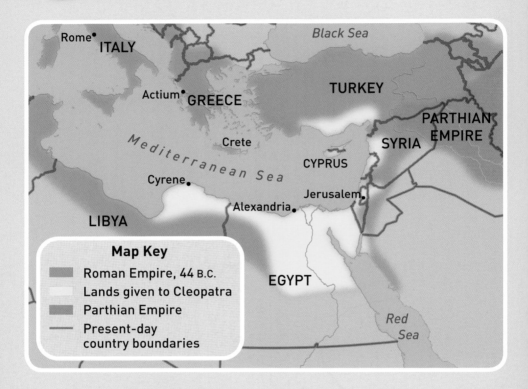

Rome• ITALY
Black Sea
TURKEY
Actium• GREECE
PARTHIAN EMPIRE
Crete
SYRIA
Mediterranean Sea
CYPRUS
Cyrene•
Jerusalem•
Alexandria•
LIBYA

Map Key
■ Roman Empire, 44 B.C.
□ Lands given to Cleopatra
■ Parthian Empire
— Present-day country boundaries

EGYPT
Red Sea

Cleopatra did not see Antony for more than three years. It was business that brought them together again. In 37 B.C., Antony was planning to attack Parthia. That area now includes the countries of Iraq and Iran. Antony needed help from Cleopatra.

She gave Antony ships, soldiers, and money for war. Antony gave Cleopatra some Roman lands in the east. They were areas that had once belonged to Egypt, but they had been lost in wars. Cleopatra wanted those lands to make Egypt strong again.

Cleopatra wanted to make Egypt strong again, as it had been many years before her time.

This detail of an 1866 painting by Alexis van Hamme shows Cleopatra sitting with Antony.

In 36 B.C., Antony went to war against Parthia. He had a large, strong army, but the leaders from Parthia had planned well. They defeated Antony's army.

In Rome, Octavian wanted more power. He tried to turn people against Antony. He said Antony gave away Roman lands to Cleopatra. He also said Antony was under Cleopatra's evil spell. Octavian wanted to go to war against Antony. He knew that was not a good idea, though. Antony still had many friends in Rome. So Octavian declared war on Egypt. He believed Antony would help Cleopatra in that fight. Octavian was right.

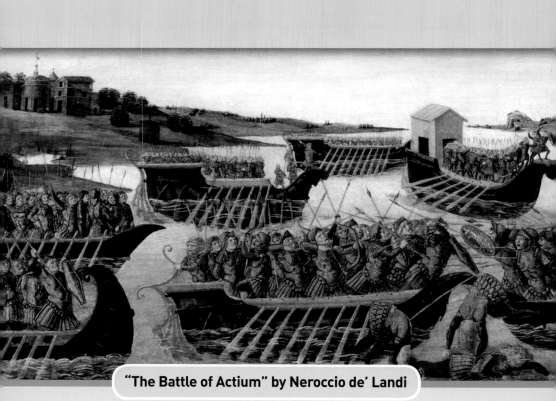

"The Battle of Actium" by Neroccio de' Landi

On September 2, 31 B.C., Antony and Cleopatra met Octavian in a sea battle near Greece. The Roman ships trapped Antony and Cleopatra's ships. Cleopatra was able to break free and Antony followed her. They sailed to Alexandria knowing Octavian would follow them. They planned to fight Octavian on land, but their soldiers gave up. They did not want to fight the strong Roman army.

It was unusual for a woman to go to war, but Cleopatra commanded her own fleet of 60 ships.

Cleopatra made plans to escape. She could begin a new life in another country. Maybe someday she could return to Egypt. That plan fell apart when soldiers burned her ships.

a wood engraving from the 1800s of Cleopatra in the Battle of Actium

The Last Queen of Egypt

A story is often told that Antony heard a rumor that Cleopatra had died. He was so upset that he stabbed himself with his sword. Then a messenger brought news. Cleopatra was still alive. Antony was carried to Cleopatra. He died in her arms.

A detail of a painting by Pompeo Batoni from the 1700s. The painting shows Cleopatra holding Mark Antony at his death.

69 B.C.

Cleopatra is born

51 B.C.

Becomes co-ruler with her brother, Ptolemy XIII

49 B.C.

Is forced out of Egypt by her brother and his advisers

This painting called "The Death of Cleopatra" is by Louis-Marie Baader.

No one knows if that story is true. It is also not clear how Cleopatra died. It is likely she took her own life because she did not want to become Octavian's prisoner. One legend says she allowed herself to be bitten by a deadly snake. Others say she took some kind of poison. Historians do know, though, that she died in August in the year 30 B.C.

48 B.C.

Meets Julius Caesar

47 B.C.

Begins her rule with her youngest brother, Ptolemy XIV

Octavian took control of Egypt. Some say he had his soldiers destroy statues and pictures of Cleopatra to get rid of any memories of the powerful queen. Others say those images were destroyed over time by war and nature.

Hundreds of years later, the section of Alexandria where Cleopatra had lived was gone. It was wiped out by earthquakes and flooding. Even now, much of it lies in the Mediterranean Sea. But Cleopatra's legend lives on. More than 2,000 years later, her story is still being told. Yet much of her life remains a mystery.

44 B.C.

Julius Caesar is killed

41 B.C.

Meets Mark Antony

37 B.C.

Gets back lands that once belonged to Egypt

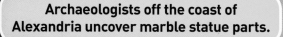

Archaeologists off the coast of Alexandria uncover marble statue parts.

An archaeologist searches for Cleopatra's tomb in the Osiris Temple ruins.

The top of a granite colossus is brought to the water's surface in Aboukir Bay.

31 B.C.

Is defeated by Octavian in a sea battle

30 B.C.

Dies in August

QUIZ WHIZ

How much do you know about Cleopatra? After reading this book, probably a lot! Take this quiz and find out.
Answers are at the bottom of page 45.

**Cleopatra was born in
_____.**

A. Greece
B. Syria
C. Egypt
D. Rome

One thing we know about Cleopatra is _____.

A. how she looked
B. that she liked movies
C. that she liked to dance
D. that she was smart

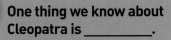

A barge is a _____.

A. musical instrument
B. game played in Egypt
C. roll of paper for writing
D. long, flat boat

4

In 48 B.C., _____ helped Cleopatra win back the throne from her brother Ptolemy XIII.

A. Ptolemy XII
B. Julius Caesar
C. Octavian
D. Alexander the Great

The name Cleopatra means _____.

A. glory of her father
B. queen of Egypt
C. leader of a nation
D. bright star

5

6

In 32 B.C., Octavian declared war on _____.

A. Mark Antony
B. Egypt
C. Syria
D. Alexander the Great

Hundreds of years after Cleopatra died, much of the area where she had lived was destroyed by _____.

A. fire
B. high winds
C. earthquakes and flooding
D. war

7

Answers: 1) C, 2) D, 3) D, 4) B, 5) A, 6) B, 7) C

Glossary

ADVISER: a person who gives advice about what should be done

DEFEAT: to win a victory over someone

EMPIRE: a group of countries or areas under the rule of one government

RUMOR: information not proved to be true

SCHOLAR: a person who studies and learns a lot about something

CO-RULER: someone who rules together with another

DECLARE: announce or say

LEGEND: a story from the past believed by many

LOYAL: faithful or trusted

SCROLL: a roll of writing material used before books were invented

SENATE: the group that made laws in Rome

Index